Make
Your Smart Baby
Super Smart

The Wisdom of Smart Parents

STEPHN LAU

DEDICATION

This book is dedicated to my daughter and her family.
May God bless them, as well as all parents
who make every effort to make their children smart and wise.

CONTENTS

THE AUTHOR'S NOTE

Writing and painting have always been my life passions. I simply like to express my thoughts in words and with colors.

I decided to write this book after knowing that my daughter would become a mother. First and foremost, I would like to tell her how I raised her, as well as to share my past experience with other parents.

I still reminisce that long-ago experience, in particular, my effort in raising my daughter. I learned how to ride a bike so that I could teach her how to ride one. I knew how to float but did not know how to breathe under water; I taught myself how to swim in order to teach her swimming. I took up some piano lessons so that I could fiddle with my fingers on the keyboard while she was practicing her piano lessons. I brushed up my rusty French so that I could help her with her French lessons. I taught her Chinese, one of the most difficult languages in the world; she could recognize more than 500 Chinese words when she was just five-years old. Most importantly, I taught her how to read; she could read when she was two-and-half-years old, and I even wrote a book "How to Teach Children to Read" based on the games and exercises I used to teach her reading skills.

I strongly believe that parents who are passionate about their children's learning experience can accomplish almost anything with their children, and the sky is the limit.

Let me tell you that the reward is nondescript. In the first few years of her life, I had given her a strong foundation for her intellectual development. The payoff was immense: throughout her elementary and high school years, she was very much on her own, and I did not have to supervise her homework or her academic studies.

Stephen Lau.

ONE

THE WISDOM OF SMART PARENTS

Congratulations! You've got yourself a smart baby. Well, at least most parents tend to *think* that their babies are smart. No matter what you think, make your baby become smart, and smarter with each day passing. You *can* do that because you *are* a smart parent yourself; you wouldn't be reading this book, if you weren't wise enough.

Are you *wise*? Well, what is wisdom?

If you have wisdom, most probably your parents are also smart and wise. However, that doesn't mean that wisdom comes solely from genes. You may have wisdom because you *desire* to be wise; that is, you want to know more, and the more you know, the wiser you may have become.

If that be the case, then is wisdom closely related to knowledge acquisition? Well, not exactly. Wisdom is more than just being knowledgeable: it is the capability of the mind to see things as they really are, and not as what they may seem to be, or are supposed to be. To illustrate, if you place a baby in front of a mirror, at first the baby may think that it is *another* baby in the mirror. But, soon enough, the baby will

1

find out that it is just his or her own reflection in the mirror. Likewise, many of us may *think* that we are who we are; however, with true wisdom, we will perceive who we *really* are, and not who we *wish* we were. Wisdom helps us separate the truths from the half-truths about ourselves or just about anything. That is why the path to wisdom involves asking many probing questions about self and others. Therefore, it is important to teach and train your child to ask questions as often as possible.

My Reflection

Asking questions was one of the many first things that I taught my daughter when she was a child. I remember once she asked me *why* her shadow was always following her. I was amazed at how observant as well as how inquisitive she was. Even now, her husband comments that she always asks questions about this and about that.

Asking questions activates brain cells, and thereby instrumental in promoting brain development and enhancing intelligence. Encourage your baby to ask questions.

Remember, as adults, we have utilized less than 20 percent of our brain cells; there is still plenty of room left for enhancement. All in all, wisdom is the mental capability to see the truths through self-intuition.

Being clever or intelligent, on the other hand, is the capability to acquire appropriate and relevant knowledge, and then apply it to solving problems in everyday life situations. If you are clever, you may have acquired the skills to put things together because you are quick to learn and understand how things work. However; being clever or intelligent doesn't necessarily mean that you must be wise. Being knowledgeable means knowing *what* to do, and being wise means knowing *when* and *how* to do it in different circumstances to suit one's unique self and purpose.

Being smart is the first step towards becoming clever or intelligent. Being smart is becoming knowledgeable, which provides the raw materials for intelligence and wisdom: it has much more to do with understanding the *how*. One doesn't become knowledgeable overnight. It is a long process of acquisition of information that requires learning and training, as well as time and effort. As soon as the baby's brain develops in the mother's womb, start touching and talking to it—and that is *how* a baby becomes smart even before it arrives into this world. The more you stimulate the brain cells, the smarter the baby becomes. When the baby comes into this world, continue nonstop your daily effort to stimulate his brain to make your baby smarter. Remember, the baby's brain is like a blank sheet of paper; the more you fill it up with knowledge and information, the smarter the baby will become.

My Reflection

I had spent much time and energy in making my daughter knowledgeable when she was a baby, a toddler, and a child. Now, is she smart? Yes, I think so. Is she intelligent? Well, I would imagine so: she is now an attorney. Then, is she *wise*? *That* I don't know. Wisdom has to do with *how* she is living her life, *how* she is going to raise her baby, and *how* she is going to face her new life challenges ahead, especially now that she has her own family. Wisdom is something that she has to self-intuit—something that cannot be taught. The parents' role is to make the child smart, which is the first step, just as **Lao Tzu**, the ancient Chinese sage, once said: "A journey of a thousand miles begins with the first step." Making your baby smart is the first big step that you can and should take, as well as the first gift that you can give to your baby. I took my first big step, and now it is my daughter's turn to take her first big step. The journey towards wisdom is long and winding, with many detours and even missteps. Hopefully, she will find her way and reach her wisdom destination.

Yes, you can teach and train your baby to become smarter. You can help your baby develop his brain, and you can even show your baby *how* to think. However, you may or may not be able to make your baby become wise: as a parent, you can only provide the tools, the raw materials, and, of course, the best wishes; the rest is up to your baby when he grows up.

TWO

UNDERSTANDING THE BASICS

Understanding *how* the brain functions and develops is important.

Brain cells develop and function as soon as they receive data from the surrounding through the five sensory organs—ears, eyes, mouth, nose, and skin; that is, hearing, seeing, tasting, smelling, and touching. The development and sharpness of these organs depend a great deal on the amount as well as the intensity of stimuli that they receive.

There are billions of brain cells, and they are like blank sheets of paper to be filled up with data obtained from the five sensory organs. They gradually become the brain, the physical organ of the body, which is responsible for thinking, often referred to as the mind.

The mind serves to control and coordinate mental and physical actions, including thoughts and feelings, as well as beliefs and attitudes. Over time, thinking will continue to develop and shape the mind, turning it into two major components—the conscious mind, and the subconscious mind. The former *selectively* controls the data input; the latter *involuntarily* and *indiscriminately* takes in all the data received. The truth of the matter is that the subconscious mind dominates the conscious mind. In other words, one's conscious mind may want to do one thing, but one's subconscious mind may instruct one to do another thing, and one may end up doing the other thing, which may be quite different from what one originally intended. Therefore, it is important to provide the right and appropriate data to the baby, because the mind of the baby is not mature enough to separate the truths from the half-truths or untruths. In other words, a baby's perceptions are permanently stored in his subconscious mind.

Remember, in the beginning, the baby's brain is not fully developed. Speed up its development through enhancing its five senses.

UNDERSTANDING YOUR BABY'S VISION

Even before birth, babies can see: they can tell what is light and what is dark. After birth, their vision improves significantly when they see shapes by following their lines. At first, they can see only within 8 to 12 inches, and they see only black, white, and gray. When they are several weeks old, they may begin to perceive their first primary color—red. Progressively, they learn how to use their eyes to see what they want to see by following moving objects. Then, they begin to learn their "binocular vision," which is coordinating and seeing with both eyes. Babies should develop their normal vision, which includes eye-hand coordination, within the first several weeks and months.

UNDERSTANDING YOUR BABY'S HEARING

Hearing is the 1st step towards language learning.

Therefore, it is important to identify and address any hearing problem by having a hearing screening test right after birth.

Babies have different responses to sounds, depending on their own temperament; more sensitive babies are more reactive to sounds; calmer babies are less reactive.

Around two months, babies begin to respond to familiar voices by making vowel sounds like *ohh*. At about four months, babies start to look for the source of a sound, and by six months they try to imitate sounds. By eight months, they babble and respond to changes in the tone of voice. By twelve months, babies may be able to say single words like "ma-ma" and "da-da."

The baby's brain continues to respond to complex sounds and attach different meanings to different sounds heard. Your baby will continue to use hearing to make sense of the world and to learn to communicate with sounds.

UNDERSTANDING YOUR BABY'S SKIN

The baby's skin is most sensitive to touch. Tactile sensations are responsible for the connection between the skin and the sympathetic nervous system; these nerves regulate heart, blood circulation, lungs, and other internal organs.

Therefore, it is important to touch the baby while breast feeding or changing diapers by touching and massaging his toes and fingers.

UNDERSTANDING YOUR BABY'S
SENSE OF TASTE AND SMELL

Most newborns will eat every two to three hours around the clock.

By the end of the first month, babies may develop an eating and sleeping pattern, but don't impose it on your baby. At this age, your baby should be fed whenever it shows signs of hunger.

Most babies have developed a sense of taste. In fact, newborns seem to have more taste buds than adults do. Sensitivity to sweet and bitter tastes is present at birth, but babies' reactions to salty foods don't come until about five months.

Babies use their sense of smell right from the start and can localize odors. Studies have shown that five-day-old newborns will turn towards a pad soaked with breast milk, indicating that they can smell it, and a few days later they demonstrate a preference for the smell of their mom's milk.

THREE

KNOWING THE BABY, KNOWING THE SELF

Understanding the basics is the first step towards making your baby smarter. The first few weeks after the birth of your baby are the time of trial and error, as well as of delight and discovery. If the baby is your first-born child, you will soon discover a new dimension in your relationship with your baby. This new relationship begins to demand your time that comprises energy and effort. Your baby's rapid development and quick responsiveness begin to enhance your own confidence and competency to confront the new challenges of parenthood.

Knowing your baby is important, but knowing the self is equally, if not more, important because the latter determines what type of parenthood you may fall into, as well as the type of child your baby will ultimately become.

KNOWING THE BABY

Observing and Bonding

Your baby grows incredibly fast. Observing your baby's unique personality development is critically important. In general, babies may be grouped into three types: the easy, the slow, and the difficult.

If your baby is "easy," congratulations! You must have done an excellent job throughout your pregnancy. If your baby happens to be "slow" or even "difficult," don't get disheartened; you just need more energy and effort to help your baby turn around to live up to his fullest potentials and to reach his personal best.

How do you know which classification your baby may fall into during the first few weeks?

For one thing, there are no hard-and-fast rules governing each classification. Just do your best to observe your baby's behavior, personality, and temperament.

Types of Baby

- Easy Babies

  Easy babies usually eat and sleep well, and they are generally very responsive to your attention and the environment. In addition, they do not cry that often, and are less irritable.

- Slow Babies

  Slow babies take time to warm up, as well as to respond to your attention and the environment. They generally smile less often, and require a stronger stimulus or greater attention.

- Difficult Babies

Difficult babies cry a lot during their sleep. They fuss a great deal during their waking time; they scream and struggle, and are more difficult to be comforted.

Which type does your baby fall into? Pay attention to how your baby eats and sleeps, how your baby moves his arms and legs, how your baby reacts to the environment with different sounds. Be very observant of your baby's unique behavior and personality development.

- Does your baby react strongly and quickly to different sounds?
- Is your baby eager to touch, grasp, and mouth anything within his reach?
- Is your baby easily contented?
- Is your baby moving a lot?
- Does your baby easily become restless during sleep?
- Does your baby easily become accustomed to any new stimulus?

Finding answers to the above questions may help you know the personality of your baby. For example, if you ring a bell, and your baby easily becomes accustomed to the sound of a bell—that is, without becoming startled or turning his head; that means your baby has the capability to "block out" the distraction and to concentrate on something new or specific. This is often a positive sign of early cognitive development.

Remember, nothing is set in stone: you can always help your baby grow out of any type.

Accepting and Appreciating

No matter what type your baby may fall into, it is *your* baby. Develop a gently loving approach to understand, accept, and appreciate your baby's behavior, capability, personality, and temperament. Remember, you can always improve his personality and temperament. Appreciate your baby's uniqueness is important to his personality growth. The bonding between the baby and the parents plays a pivotal role in the baby's own physical and mental development. This relationship is the groundwork for the baby's learning experience, as well as the baby's individual personality traits and abilities. If you want your baby to become super smart, always enhance this bonding and relationship.

Remember the following:

- Always create a nurturing environment in which your baby can grow cognitively.
- Learn to relax if your baby is too demanding; try to take a nap while your baby is sleeping.
- Learn to smile when approaching your screaming baby. Remember, your baby may be as miserable as you are, and he is there not to annoy you.
- Accept a difficult baby: things will change for the better.

KNOWING THE SELF

"Knowing others is intelligence.
Knowing ourselves is true wisdom.
Overcoming others is strength.

Overcoming ourselves is true power."
Lao Tzu, *"Tao Te Ching"* (chapter 33)

Lao Tzu, the ancient sage from China, rightfully said that to know one's true self is not easy: it requires profound wisdom. Sometimes we think that we know ourselves—who we really are—but in fact we don't. Asking probing and self-intuitive questions may help us get to the bottom of the truth about ourselves.

Who are you as a parent?

First and foremost, best parents are not infallible; nobody is perfect, and you are no exception.

Look back at your own childhood. You may have been influenced by *how* your parents acted towards you. There might have been positive and negative experiences. Now, your goal as a parent is to emulate the positive aspects of your parents, and to avoid repeating their mistakes.

Types of Parenting

Parenting style generally falls into three types, although there may be overlaps and variations.

- Authoritative Parents

   Authoritative parents often provide an environment of freedom and democracy. They set rules and regulations that their children must follow or obey. However, within these boundaries, children are encouraged to act, speak, and think independently without any restrain or restriction. Authoritative parents are always in control of their children, but they also encourage from their children's verbal exchange and creative thinking based on different situations and circumstances.

Authoritative parents generally produce happy, smart, and self-reliant children.

- Permissive Parenting

  Permissive parents are generally accepting and non-punitive regarding their children's attitudes and behaviors. In many ways, their children's actions and reactions, as well as their desires and impulses control and determine the parent-child relationships. The only drawbacks are that these children tend to become less self-reliant and initiating.

- Authoritarian Parenting

  Authoritarian parents are always much in control of the behaviors of their children based on their own standards; they attempt to shape the growth and development of their children. Other than obedience, there is not much room for any compromise or even flexibility. Children under authoritarian parents are generally distrustful, discontented, and withdrawn. Worse, they often become rebellious in adolescence.

The style of parenting is based on the parents' beliefs, values, personality, and upbringing. To make your baby smart, you need to give him an environment of safety, peace and harmony. Parenting, like marriage, is partnership; make sure that both of you are on the same page.

FOUR

LEARNING AND TEACHING

To make your smart baby super smart, make your home a classroom of learning and teaching. More importantly, make it safe and secure for your baby. You teach, and your baby learns; as you teach, you yourself also learn. Learning to teach and teaching to learn is a unique lifetime experience for both the parents and their children.

Your Baby's Brain

At birth, a baby's brain weighs approximately 25 percent of that of an adult. At six months, it may increase to 50 percent. At one year, a baby's brain may develop to 70 percent or more of that of an adult. At around three years, a baby's brain may become fully developed. As the baby' brain develops, the baby learns; the more it learns, the faster the brain develops. Therefore, make the most out of the first three years to maximize your baby's brain development for a smarter baby.

Through learning and teaching, you can enhance and

accelerate the growth of your baby's brain. A baby's initial body movements are based on reflexes, which can be quickly replaced by voluntary, intentional movements as soon as its trillions of brain cells begin to develop and mature. As a result, the first few years are particularly vital to the development of brain cells, providing the groundwork for intelligence.

Learning and Remembering

Learning is a process of perceiving and understanding information received by the brain. But information is useless and irrelevant unless it is easily and readily available and retrievable; in other words, information must be remembered and properly stored as memories in different compartments of the brain, which are like file cabinets in the human brain.

The Different Memory Techniques

In order for information to be properly stored by the brain, it must be experienced through its five sensory organs. Most learning involves one of three primary techniques:

- *Visual memory* involves seeing, such as studying a map or an illustration. Visual-memory learning is faster with greater confidence.
- *Auditory memory* involves hearing, such as listening to a song or lecture. Auditory-memory learning enhances the compartmentalization of complex materials.
- *Kinesthetic memory* involves doing, such as brushing teeth or swimming. Kinesthetic-memory learning is more enduring because it is more

automatic and spontaneous.

These memory techniques are critical to learning. Many of us are more efficient at one type of memory than another; for example, most of us learn best by using visual memory than by using auditory or kinesthetic memory. Having said that, if you wish your baby to have exceptional memories, develop his skills and proficiency in *all* memory techniques.

Enriched Learning and Teaching Environment

Most real learning in the first year occurs within the context of ordinary everyday life. It doesn't require formal training; it is a natural consequence of everyday experience. Be that as it may, to maximize your baby's learning potentials, you need to create an enriched learning and teaching environment. The typical American child, however, does not live in an enriched environment: he spends hours watching television or playing electronic toys; he is often engaged in self-directed play, instead of interactive and imaginative play with his parents.

An enriched learning and teaching environment for babies and children to reach their maximum intellectual potentials includes the following:

- Your baby needs to spend time in a safe, secure, and quiet environment.
- Your baby needs a dimly lit environment to see better; use only 40-watt or less light-bulbs in the nursery.
- Your baby needs freedom of movement; use the crib or playpen sparingly.
- Your baby needs age-related toys and art

materials.

- Your baby needs new things to look at all the time.
- Your baby needs regular contacts with adults, especially eye contacts.
- Your baby needs smiles, as well as friendly and affirmative words.

Is Your Baby Ready to Play and Learn?

There are some obvious physical changes and signs if your baby is good and ready to play and learn.

- Your baby needs good rest before he can play and learn. Adequate rest avoids mood swings and improves the brain function in your baby.
- If your baby wants to play and learn, his breathing is always slow and even, with a relaxed abdomen.
- Your baby sucking rate also slows down considerably.
- Your baby's attention focuses on the source of stimulation, his fingers and toes fanning with excitement towards it, as well as his pupils dilating and his eyes widening.

On the other hand, your baby may show signs of overstimulation when he cries and squirms, flailing his arms and legs, and even thrusting out his tongue.

Good parenting means providing an enriched learning environment for babies and children to learn while playing. A study conducted at the University of Chicago found out that some accomplished adults, such as distinguished athletes, musicians, mathematicians, and scientists all had parents who shared certain outlooks about enriched environment in which they were raised and reared. They all unintentionally produced a prodigy

- They all encouraged their children to play and to explore the world.
- They all stimulated and motivated their children through playing and learning.
- They were all dedicated to their own interests, and encouraged their children to do likewise, but without pushing them in that direction.
- They all supported their children's self-chosen interests, and made their passion a top priority.
- They all encouraged their children to have independent thinking, and to think for themselves through curiosity and asking questions.

The key to successful parenting is to provide an enriched environment for learning while playing, as well as for recognizing talents and potentials that may or may not be the skills and abilities you value most. Praising your baby's efforts and his accomplishments strengthens your baby's neurological connections between activity and emotional rewards, and thus instrumental in developing more interest in trying new things and experiences.

Bottom line: the more your baby enjoys spending time with you as he explores the world, the more motivated he will become, and the more he will learn. Relax, loosen up, and always look at the environment and the world through your baby's eyes, rather than those of your own. It is just that simple.

Sustained Drive and Curiosity

It is important to maintain and sustain the learning and teaching process of your baby. According to novelist **John Steinbeck**, a genius is "a child chasing a butterfly up a mountain"; let your baby's curiosity be the butterfly and let his learning environment be the mountain.

FIVE

THE DAILY DOS AND DON'TS OF PARENTS

Thomas Edison rightfully said: "Genius is one percent inspiration, and 99 percent perspiration."

This applies to both the baby and the parents. Perspiration means effort and endeavor, both of which involve consistent and considerable time consumption. Do spend time with your baby if you want him to be smart. If you are the parents who wish your baby to become a super baby—not necessarily a genius or prodigy someday—there are many things you have to do, as well as many things you shouldn't do.

Repetitions

Do repeat and repeat. Repetitions strengthen the neural pathways in your baby's brain. Do *any* activity with your baby again and yet again. Do encourage your baby to repeat his activities again and yet again.

Don't stop an activity just because your baby has already acquired the skills or learned how to do it. Repeat it not only to reinforce it but also to improve his memory skills.

Don't get bored yourself. Instead, do observe the subtle differences in the repetitions of those activities to better understand how your baby has managed and mastered those memory skills.

Stimulations

Do give your baby stimulations as many and as often as possible. Any physical stimulation enhances brain cells and motor skills development in your baby.

Do stimulate your baby's auditory sensations. Do speak in different tones: whispering and shouting (of course, don't frighten your baby). Do articulate your words slowly, syllable by syllable. Do sing to your baby, even creating your own words and rhythms.

Do touch your baby as often as possible, especially his fingers and toes.

Do create movements: exaggerated facial expressions; clapping hands; and even jumping up and down.

Do vary your stimulations, the types, as well as the duration.

Do encourage your baby to respond to your different stimulations. If he makes noises, let him. If he smiles, repeat it.

The bottom line: don't let your baby get bored; but don't over-stimulate your baby (no more than 5 minutes each time).

Toys and Play Activities

Toys play a pivotal role in the growth and development of a baby's brain.

Do buy toys that require imagination. Don't buy toys that

rely solely on batteries. Do buy toys that stimulate different senses of your baby, such as seeing, hearing, and touching.

Do buy toys that focus on role-play, letting you say: "I'll be your Mom (or Dad), and you'll be the baby." Role-play not only enhances your baby's awareness of his role in the world around but also develops his own creativity. Do have unstructured playtime with your baby: this develops your baby's language and prolongs your baby's attention span, which is critical to learning. Do engage in many role-playing games, such as "let's pretend."

Do introduce to your baby one or two new toys at a time. Don't overwhelm your baby with too many new toys. Do allow your baby to explore new toys while having access to familiar objects. Do make your baby feel secure.

Do engage in creative play activities with your baby all the time.

1 to 3 Months

Rattles, stuffed toys, unbreakable mirrors, music boxes, large rings, books with high-contrast pictures should be attached to the crib or the activity center of your baby. They should be in black and white, or with brightly colored patterns. Use these toys to engage your baby's attention and stimulation.

4 to 6 Months

Squeaky toys, building blocks, beach balls, books made of cloth are some of the popular baby toys at this age. Play peekaboo with your baby as often as possible.

7 to 9 Months

Get your baby some stuffed animals, large balls, pop-up toys, stacking blocks and toys, dolls and puppets, and squeeze toys. Play patty-cake with your baby.

10 to 12 Months

By this time, your baby may need push-and-pull toys, such as miniature cars. Be creative, and give your baby some ordinary household objects, such as empty egg cartons, bath toys, or old magazines. Play simple ball games with your baby.

One-year-old and beyond

There are many different types of toys to suit the personality of your baby: toy telephones, simple musical instruments, toys to take apart and put back together, easy jigsaw puzzles, large crayons and markers, shape sorters, finger paints, and action toys, such as fire engines. Play more outdoor games with your baby.

Many experts believe that computers can enhance cognitive development only in five-year-olds and beyond. For under-three-year-old babies, do use your discretion to determine your baby's exposure time to the computer.

The bottom line: do keep it fun; and do take a brief walk after your baby has learned something new because the neural connections formed in your baby's brain needs time for more reinforcement before he can process more new information.

Discipline

Children need discipline, including babies and toddlers. Discipline is a process of teaching your baby to be an independent being through self-control and self-regulation by establishing certain boundaries and reinforcing them so that he has a mental pattern of what he should or shouldn't do.

Studies have shown that the way parents handle discipline can affect positively or negatively the IQ of their children. Children growing up in a hostile and restrictive home tend to have a lower IQ than those who come from a loving and democratic one. Drawing the fine line may not be easy, but it is not impossible.

- Do establish discipline based on your beliefs and values.
- Do explain the rules, and why those rules are there. Do make sure your child understands them.
- Do make your instructions clear and authoritative. Don't put them in the form of a request, such as "Can you, please, stop that?"
- Don't give out too many rules at one time. Saying "No" is ineffective; your baby might even think that his name is "No."
- Do be firm. A loud "No!" or "Don't do that!" is okay with a toddler or child; for a baby, use sign language.
- Don't spank your toddler. Why not? It only shows you've lost control yourself, and you're also showing your child that it's okay to use force to dominate others. Don't let your child model your improper conduct.
- Don't inflict any physical punishment. Don't shake your baby or toddler. There are many instances of death resulting from shaking babies and toddlers. Shaken babies may experience brain damage, resulting in mental retardation and even blindness.

- Do be consistent with your reaction to certain unwanted behavior. Any inconsistent discipline only confuses your child.
- Do discipline immediately, and not after the fact.
- Do give your child a good reason to obey, such as "Go to bed now, and I'll tell you a story." But don't make it bribery.
- Do show yourself as a loving and affirming parent. Do offer reassurance to your child that you still love him even though his behavior may be unacceptable, requiring discipline.

Discipline plays a pivotal role in the emotional and intellectual development of your baby, toddler, and child. Remember this: babies are egocentric, and they think the world revolves around them. Introduce discipline at around nine months of age, and not before that.

Emotional Development

The first three years are critical to emotional intelligence and intellectual development that ultimately affect and shape the adult life of your baby.

Emotional Intelligence

Emotional intelligence is the use of mental skills to understand, perceive, and explain certain human emotions and feelings in order to promote better thinking and to enhance greater cognitive activities. Most importantly, it helps an adult to manage his or her own emotions in a positive way—this is vital to living a happy life through better relationships and greater understanding of others.

Building emotional health and personal identity of your baby is the groundwork of his subsequent emotional intelligence.

Do give your baby the best first three years of his life. Do understand that your interactions with your baby define his expectations of the world, and shape his attitudes towards life in general.

According to famous psychologist **Erik Erikson**, *trust* holds the key to openness to new experiences, and new opportunities for leaning; your baby's trust stems from being loved and nurtured, as well as feeling safe and secure, in the first few years of his life. Do give your baby that love and sense of security. Remember, you can never turn back the clock.

A baby's feeling of trust is built upon good bonding between the baby and the parents. These are some of the dos and don'ts to build your baby's trust:

- Do establish direct physical contact: do make every effort to snuggle your baby as much and as often as possible. According to research studies, babies at age two, having had better bonding with their parents, demonstrate better social and problem-solving skills, as well as more creativity in their play.
- Do spend time with your baby. One interesting study found that one common characteristic of all who did well in the Scholastic Aptitude Tests (SATs): they all ate dinner with their parents on a regular basis. If you must go to work, make sure that your spouse or the grandparents can spend some time with your baby.
- Do learn to read and interpret your baby's signals

to communicate his needs to you, and respond appropriately. Do teach him sign language (see pages 42-47) so that he can communicate with you even before he can speak.

- Do meet *all* your baby's needs. You can spoil a toddler or a child, but you can never spoil a baby. Secure emotions enhance the development of emotional intelligence in the brain. Do make every effort to meet his needs to help his brain develop his emotional intelligence at an early age.

- Do create a stress-free environment for your baby. Don't argue or fight in front of your baby. Stress increases your baby's hormone cortisol, which can make your baby become anxious, impulsive, and hyperactive later on as he grows up.

- Do provide affirmative messages to your baby. Before three years old, your baby will instinctively absorb all messages you send him, and will automatically internalize them in his subconscious mind. Repeat and repeat as often as possible affirmative messages, such as "You're a smart kid" or "You're super smart; you can do anything you want to." Do make use of this timeframe to help him create a positive self-image. Don't say any damaging remark no matter how frustrating you are with his behavior; he will remember your words for the rest of his life even though you may not mean what you say.

- Do teach your two-year-old (known as "terrible two") self-control; his personality may have become defiant and uncooperative because he is learning and struggling with his own self-control. Do respond with a clear and definitive "No!"

followed by a calm explanation; this may help your child understand why he cannot always have his way. Don't criticize or physically intervene his action while losing your temper; you may be cultivating his defiance towards authority figures.

- Do teach your baby orderliness, which is putting things where they belong. For example, you can show your toddler where to put his toys or how to clean up after playtime. Orderliness will help him see how the world works later as he grows up. Your child needs to get the satisfaction from doing things himself, such as cleaning and tidying his room or playroom. Don't spoil your child by doing everything yourself.

Intellectual Development

You are the most important role model for your baby's intellectual development. If you like to read, your child will learn to read at any early age.

My Reflection

Wanting my daughter to have the best intellectual development, I began teaching her how to read as early as she was eight months old. Surprisingly, she learned how to read as soon as she was thirty months old. Before long, she could read faster than I. My point is that any intellectual development has to be cultivated and nurtured. If you want your baby to be an early reader, spend time reading with her.

Emotional intelligence is essentially awareness of one's emotions and feelings, as well as those of others. Likewise, intellectual development in a baby is contingent on the parental awareness of the emotional development of the baby. Do become aware of your baby's development, which is a reflection of his own emotional growth; the following usually occurs within the first year:

- Your baby begins to show sensitivity to loud sounds and bright lights. Do hold and snuggle him more.
- Your baby begins to recognize your voice and turn to make eye contact with you. Do look at your baby more often.
- Your baby begins to develop his social smile. Do reward it with your warm smile.
- Your baby begins to enjoy the company of other people. Do have people, such as grandparents, around your baby.
- Your baby begins to imitate movements and facial expressions. Do make movements with your hands and fingers, as well as with your eyes and mouth.
- Your baby begins to laugh when playing to express his pleasure. Do laugh while playing with your baby.
- Your baby begins to raise his arms to be picked up. Do pick up your baby.
- Your baby begins to complain when confined to his crib or playpen. Do let your baby out.

All of the above may develop in your baby before age-one. Do try to meet all your baby needs to comply with his emotional development, thereby instrumental in enhancing his intellectual development.

Movements and Motor Skills

Your baby grows up with movements and motor skills. A healthy baby will crawl, walk, and run—but at a pace based on his brain and neurological development. You can never force your baby to grow up faster than nature intends. Don't expect too much; any unrealistic expectation from you, such as saying "You *can* walk!" may frustrate your baby, sending him a message of negative emotion instead.

Do touch and massage your baby from head to toes. Regular touching and stroking will stimulate your baby's neuro-muscular development.

Do encourage your baby's sensory and motor development by strengthening his neck and shoulder muscles. Do put your baby on his tummy so that he will learn to lift his head and shoulders, as well as to rotate his upper body and roll over. But don't let your baby sleep on his tummy.

Do play with your baby to stimulate and strengthen his motor skills.

Do help your baby open and close his hands, especially by the second month when his reflexes begin to fade.

Do hold your baby in a standing position on a firm surface to let him push down his legs (at around the third month).

Do help your baby sit up (at around the fourth month) and balance.

Do help your baby grab his feet and put them in his mouth when lying down.

Do help your baby hold an object and put it in his mouth.

31

Do encourage your baby to reach out for an object while sitting in balance.

Do help your baby support his entire weight on his legs (at around sixth to the seventh month).

Do encourage your baby to crawl towards you (at around the eighth month).

As your baby's muscles strengthen, he may start walking and standing without any support before he is one-year-old. It is important to stimulate his motor skills and encourage his actions to strengthen his muscles.

The bottom line: let your baby develop in his own unique way and at his own pace. As a parent, you can enhance his motor skills and provide more opportunities for him to do what he wants to do.

SIX

SHARPENING SMARTNESS

Super smart babies often demonstrate multi-faceted intelligence in different areas, such as arts and music, math and science, and languages. Therefore, it is important to sharpen your baby's smartness in all these different areas in order to bring out his full potentials.

Artistic Skills and Musical Talents

As a parent, do explore and develop your baby's artistic and musical talents and potentials, which play a pivotal role in enhancing the development of creativity brain cells in your baby.

Arts

Do encourage your baby to pick up a crayon, but don't if he is still chewing it in his mouth. Do let him express himself through representational art on a blank sheet of paper. This may form the foundation of your baby's creativity and imagination, which are the main components of smartness and intelligence.

Do pick up a paintbrush yourself, and show your baby how you express your creativity (even though you may not be versatile in art or painting). Don't let your baby see your own frustration with your artistic expression. Don't even praise his artwork; instead, praise his effort (the explanation is that he should not be given the impression that comparing his artwork with that of others, or even with that of his own, may inhibit his creativity). Don't express your favoritism of one piece of his artwork over another, unless he asks for your opinion. Do ask your baby to express his comments on his own artwork, and do ask him why he likes it, meanwhile helping him to say something like "This color is good."

Music

All children were born with musical abilities, but most of them were not given the opportunities to cultivate and develop their innate gifts after birth. After spending months in the mother's womb, listening to the regular and rhythmic heartbeats of the mother, the baby's brain is smart-wired to the rhythm of music.

During the months of pregnancy, your baby inside the womb had already experienced many different types of auditory stimulations—such as gurgles, pulses, heartbeats, and digestive noises, including human voices—that have formed the groundwork for your baby's inherent interests in and preferences for rhythmic sounds, not to mention his possible inborn talents in music.

According to studies, babies have a tendency to increase their sucking rate of their pacifiers with rhythmic music or noise. In addition, babies respond well to changes in pitch and tempo even at any early age. Furthermore, music can enhance babies' brain development in terms of science, mathematics, and spatial relations. A case in point, **Albert Einstein** started playing the violin at the age of five because his mother was a devoted musician.

Soft background music can improve your baby's moods, and thereby enhancing his learning abilities by facilitating his brain to acquire new information. Studies have also shown that music helps babies not only gain weight but also develop motor coordination through relaxation. Research conducted at the University of California, Irvine, found out that formal training on the keyboard and singing significantly increased spatial intelligence in children. Some day-care centers and preschools in the United States are even obligated to play classical music because it can build and increase brain power over the long haul.

Given the many enormous benefits of music on the brain development of your baby, do continually provide in your baby's living and play environment soft classical music in the background. Choose your music from Bach, Beethoven, Brahms, and Mozart. If you can play a musical instrument, play it in front of your baby; if you cannot, sing before him. Always use music to engage his attention or dance to the music.

Math and Science Capabilities

Spatial Thinking

Spatial thinking is an important aspect of a baby's overall intelligence because visual spatial attention can lead to the development of an eye for detail, as well as a photographic memory, which are essential elements in the development of intelligence. According to research studies, accelerated spatial thinking is the stepping stone to ultimate enhanced IQ. Recent research has suggested that a baby's visual spatial attention ability is a precursor of his reading skills. Although it is a general belief that males have better spatial skills than females, experts believe that spatial intelligence can be improved in both sexes with practice, especially at an early age.

Timeline

How soon can you teach your baby spatial thinking or just anything for that matter?

First and foremost, there are no hard-and-fast rules governing the milestones of learning.

According to common belief, the accepted age is 18-month-old for leaning colors, 24-month-old for leaning shapes, and 36-month-old for learning letters and numbers. But don't let your mind be preconditioned by any timeline.

Remember, the first three years are most important for the development of your baby's brain, and anything that your baby is exposed to will be imprinted in his brain as memories, which are the raw materials with which he can build his intelligence later in life. So, a baby's learning capability boils down to three things: *time*, *effort*, and *opportunities*. Do the parents have the time? Are they willing to put in their effort to teach? Do they create the opportunities of learning for their baby?

Can babies *really* learn visual spatial thinking at any early age?

Learning is no more than repetition, repetition, and repetition. Keep on repeating the visual as well as the auditory input until it is registered in the baby's subconscious mind. The timeline is not that important as long as the baby's sensory organs are sharp and proficient enough to receive the input from the repetition. When and how the baby is going to internalize and understand the information is at the discretion of the baby. It is just like that you can make your baby smart, but you may not be able to make him wise; still, you have to make him smart in the first place.

The story of **Helen Keller** may illustrate the above. She was the first deaf-blind person to earn a Bachelor of Arts degree. Keller's teacher taught her sign language, and she mastered it. But, in the beginning, she had no idea that every sign referred to a particular object; she could not understand the relationship between the signs and the objects until one day when she perceived their subtle relationships—it was total awakening and enlightenment for her. Likewise, you can teach your baby visual spatial intelligence until one day he can understand the concept and then relate it to what he has already learned and mastered.

Spatial Intelligence

Spatial intelligence is the mental concept of the relationships between things: differences in colors, patterns, positions, shapes, and sizes of different objects.

Encourage your baby to pay more attention to spatial information, while using a lot of spatial language yourself to enhance his visual spatial capability.

For example, while showing your baby two balls of the same color but different in size, say "BIG ball" and "SMALL ball"; repeat and repeat them in different positions. Your baby is hearing three words "big," "small," and "ball" while seeing three different things "big ball," "small ball," and "color of the balls." Through repetition, the data is recorded in your baby's memory. However, at first, the data will not make any sense to your baby until he can relate the sound "ball" to the object, and he knows what a "ball" looks like; as soon as he understands colors, he will then be able to grasp the more abstract spatial concept of "big" and "small."

In the same way, you can teach your baby colors with M&M's, as well as sorting them into different categories based on different colors; sorting out is also another important aspect of spatial learning.

You don't have to wait till your baby goes to preschool to learn spatial thinking. Teach your baby spatial language, and repeat it again and over again, and let him understand the concept when he is mentally good and ready. Don't push him! Be creative in teaching while playing with your baby; always make it fun and interesting. Remember, your baby learns through seeing and hearing, and remembering. How your baby is going to process the information received is beyond your control. Just do what you need to do as a smart parent to make your smart baby super smart.

Counting

Teach your baby the mathematic concept of numbers, even long before he can speak.

Show your baby your one finger, and say: "ONE." Then show him your two fingers and say "TWO." If your baby begins to show his interest in language, he will look at your mouth and watch how you articulate clearly and slowly those words. Repeat the process with two similar objects, such as two balls, saying "ONE" and "TWO." At first, you baby may think that the sounds of the two words refer to the balls and the fingers. But, as soon as he knows what "balls" and "fingers" are, he will then perceive the abstract concept of numbers. Then proceed to counting other numbers, and play some simple board games, during which he learns to read the numbers on the dice as he moves his playing piece over the board.

The bottom line: expose your baby to the mathematic concept, and let him relate or understand the concept when he is mentally ready. Recognition of objects is the first step, and understanding the mathematic concept of numbers will follow suit.

To illustrate, "Chaser" is the name of the dog belonging to a retired psychologist **John Pilley**, who has successfully trained his dog to recognize over one thousand toys or items by their name and retrieve them at his command. It was shown on TV that Chaser has the largest tested memory of any non-human animal. If a dog can do it, a smart baby may have the super memory to remember everything. All he needs to do is to harness his mental skills to put everything in the right order through mental perception, and then relate them to some abstract concepts he has experienced or has been exposed to—this mental visualization and subsequent profound understanding is a testament to his intelligence.

My Reflection

When my daughter was only eight months old, I began to teach her how to read. One of the early stages to master reading skills is the recognition of words in relation to objects. That was how I started the teaching: as I was carrying her in my arms, I pointed to a TV set, and said: "TEE-VEE" She looked at how I slowly articulated the word, while pointing to the TV. I repeated the process every day. Before long, when I uttered the word "TEE-VEE," she immediately turned her head to the direction of the TV without my pointing at it. If I could do it, you can do it too.

Math and science are interesting and fun if you allow your baby to experience the natural world firsthand. Don't feel you must teach your baby specific facts and scientific principles; instead, let him explore and experience everything firsthand. Do teach him the specific skills of awareness and asking questions. Let your baby discover the answers through his own experience.

Learning Languages

Every baby is programmed to communicate to have his or her needs met. The human brain is inherently wired to learn language to express such needs and wants. Some babies develop their language skills early, while others much later. Developing language skills takes time. No matter what, all babies want to communicate with their parents, even though their development of speech may lag way behind. Feeling frustrated, they often resort to crying and screaming.

Baby Sign Language

Consciously or unconsciously, we all use simple signs, such as waving our hands with "bye-bye" and clapping our hands to express our delight. Baby sign language is just simple gesturing to communicate with your baby. Your baby's hand-eye coordination develops much faster than his speech. Prior to about 12-18 months, your baby may not have acquired his motor skills and muscles of the mouth and tongue to articulate intelligent words; whereas, by 6-7 months, he may have much better control of larger muscles, such as his hands, to start his own sign language to communicate with you.

It is a misconception that learning sign language will delay a baby's ability to learn his spoken language; quite the contrary, learning sign language will accelerate the process of learning the spoken language. As a matter of fact, your baby will drop his sign language as soon as he learns how to say the word for that sign. Learning sign language is a bridge to developing your baby's speech, expression, and overall communication skills. So, do teach your baby sign language, allowing him to communicate with you long before he can use his speech.

Benefits

Baby sign language is proven to enhance babies' brain development in addition to its many other benefits:

- Your baby can communicate with you before he masters his own language skills. Research has shown that children of deaf parents are able to communicate earlier than children of hearing parents.
- Your baby gets a smart start with increased vocabulary and more advanced cognitive skills to enhance his subsequent speech development.
- Your baby's sign language helps your baby become more sociable because his brain is smart-wired to reading the body language of others.
- Your baby's sign language smart-wires his brain for solving-problem ability.
- You know exactly what your baby wants without second guessing.
- A research study indicated that eight-year-olds with baby sign language training as infants had an average IQ 12 points above those without the training.
- Your baby has a better bonding with you.

Teach your baby simple signs for basic activities, such as diaper changing, eating, milking, and sleeping. Being able to communicate his needs avoids a lot of frustrations and crying. Remember, your baby is unable to learn if he is feeling frustrated, uncomfortable, and insecure.

Simple Steps

Start with teaching your baby some simple signs. Your baby will want to mimic your signs. Once your baby signs back, then praise him, and repeat until he masters them. As your baby gets better at signing, then proceed to teaching him a few more signs to increase his vocabulary.

- Say the word clearly and slowly, demonstrate the sign—repeat and repeat—in relation to what you are doing, for example, changing diaper, drinking milk, or eating.
- Do praise and encourage your baby, even if he is signing incorrectly.
- Be creative in using signs for different objects and situations that your baby enjoys.

Simple Signs

- Teach your baby simple signs from the very beginning of his life. Your baby may not know what you are doing, but perform those simple signs until you have mastered them, and they have become second nature to you.
- Teach your baby the sign of "mommy":

- Extend and spread out your fingers (of the right or left hand) with your pinky finger pointing forward, and your thumb touching your chin.
- Smile, and gently say "Mommy" slowly and clearly every time you approach your baby.

"Mommy" Sign

Teach your baby the sign of "daddy," which is similar to that of "mommy," except the position of the hand is different in that the thumb is touching the eyebrow instead of the chin.

"Daddy" Sign

Teach your baby the sign of "hunger":

- Make your hand into the shape as if you were holding some food in your hand, with your palm facing you.
- Place your hand near your mouth as if you were eating the food in your hand.
- Then slowly move your hand downward into your tummy, while saying the word "hungry."
- Repeat the process.

Teach your baby the sign of "eat."

"Eat" Sign

Teach your baby the sign of "more":

- Use both hands with fingers and thumbs together as if you were picking up a little food in each hand.
- Bring your hands together and then separate them repeatedly, while saying: "More!" or asking the question: "Do you want *more*?"

Use the sign of "more" not just while your baby is eating, but also while he is playing or being tickled. You can also use the sign of "more" to teach your baby question-and-answer by changing your tone of voice.

"More" Sign

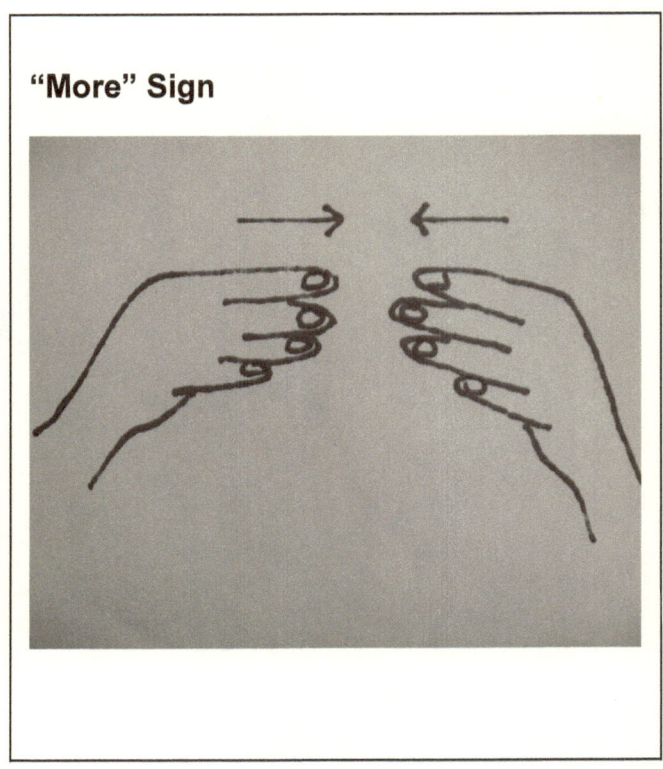

Teach your baby the sign of "play."

- Tap your gathered fingers to tips.
- Extend thumbs and little pinky fingers of both closed fists.
- Turn both hands at wrists.

Use this "play" sign whenever you play with your baby. Encourage your baby to use this sign when he wants to play too.

"Play" Sign

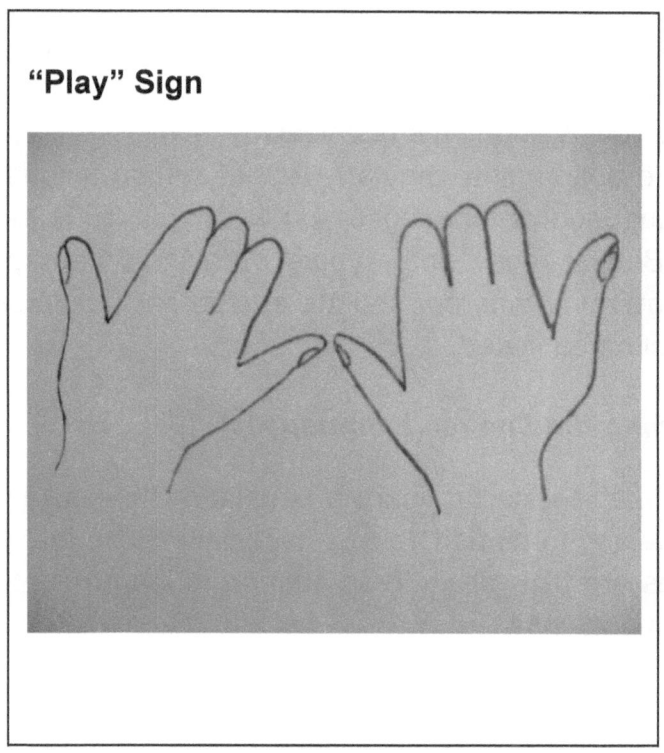

You can create your own signs as long as you are consistent. Use signs like "blowing kisses" or "waving bye-bye."

Learning More Than One Language

Given that different languages have their uniquely different sounds or phonemes for uniquely different words, expose your baby to different languages if you wish your baby to become bi-lingual or even multi-lingual. Learning more than one language always sharpens your baby's smartness in language learning. However, it is important that the exposure of your baby to those unique sounds occurs on a regular basis within the first twelve months. The explanation is that your baby may lose his ability to distinguish the differences between the sounds of his mother tongue and the uniquely different sounds of other languages if he is not already exposed to them on a regular basis during the first year.

The bottom line: regularly repeat certain unique sounds of the language or languages you wish your baby to learn later on. Before age one, your baby has no problem in distinguishing different sounds in different languages, and he will not be confused.

Learning the Spoken Language

All babies start to learn a language while still in the womb by listening to human voices, especially those of their parents. Babies are biologically programmed to learn how to speak by imitating sounds.

Ways to Enhance the Learning Process

The intellectual development of your baby is closely related to his physical development, in particular, his motor abilities. Increase and improve his motor skills:

- In the first month, try to open and loosen his fists so that he will learn the grasping reflex, which is critical to holding objects to learn. Open his fists, and place your fingers into them. Also, open his fists and close them with your hands.
- In the second month, place various bright objects within his hands' movements. Don't place them directly into his hands; instead, guide them directly into his unclenched fists so that the grasping becomes incidental.

Sharpening your baby's sensory perception is a further step to enhance his learning process:

- In the third month, promote his visual perception by teaching and training your baby to follow objects with his eyes with increasing speed and various ranges of their movements.
- In the third month, show your baby the coordination of sight and hearing, that is, the connection between what he sees and what he hears. Provide your baby with plenty of auditory experiences, such as different human voices, songs, music, and clapping hands, among others.

All babies have an inborn ability to imitate, especially, their parents. Imitation is a prerequisite in language learning. Stimulate your baby to imitate:

- Around five to six months, induce self-imitation by banging a toy to create a noise. Your baby may repeat his self-imitation if he is able to make the connection between his action and the noise.
- Reinforce his self-imitation by repeating the action yourself.

Develop your baby's thinking to understand the relationship between cause and effect; that is, how to act on an object to produce a certain effect.

- At around seven months, show your baby how a certain action will produce a certain expected result, such as squeezing a certain toy to create a certain sound. It should be apparent that he expects the result and that the result is the reason he is taking the required action.

- Show your baby how he can get his toy by pulling a string that is attached to it.

At around seventh to eighth month, your baby may begin to recognize objects by making some unintelligible sounds as if he were *naming* them. This is the beginning of his passive speech. Teach your baby passive speech:

- Show your baby that everything has a name by naming it while pointing at it.
- If your baby mumbles, give him an interesting new toy. Let him play with it for a while, and then take it away. If he mumbles again, give him the same piece of toy to stimulate his mumbling.
- If your baby mumbles, lift him high in the air (he will enjoy it), and smile at him. If he mumbles again, repeat the lifting up to induce him to mumble more.

By the end of the first year, your baby should be ready for active speech when he understands simple sentences about everyday situations and objects he is familiar with. Teach your baby active speech:

- Encourage your baby to repeat syllables several times. If your baby says "ma," then repeat "ma-ma-ma-ma." Also, teach your baby to link two different syllables, such as "ba-ma" and "da-ba."
- Teach your baby active words, which are related to actions, objects, and people he already knows. Active words are best learned from passive ones, that is, those that your baby already understands.

Alphabets are excellent for learning vocabulary.

- Make your baby articulate a certain syllable before giving him his food or favorite toy.
- Use "self-talk" to teach your baby words related to activities. Describe your activities and feelings; for example, say "I am giving you this teddy bear."
- Use "parallel talk" to describe what your baby is doing; for example, "You are drinking your milk."

Begin Your Baby's Learning Process

Begin the journey of learning process. Take the first step and begin the journey with your baby, providing him with a compass and a roadmap. The journey may be long and winding with many detours and sidesteps. The final destination is up to your baby. You can make him smart, but you cannot make him wise; you can give him intelligence, but you cannot give him wisdom. As a parent, help your baby begin his learning process.

- Talk to your baby as much as possible. Researchers found out that babies whose parents were verbal had a much wider and more diverse vocabulary than babies whose parents seldom spoke to them.
- Increase your baby's verbal communication with frequent eye-contacts, more facial expressions, and expressive gestures. According to research studies, babies move their arms to match the cadence of what they are hearing, and such movements are critical to grasping the rhythm of language, leading to early verbal comprehension.
- Speak to your baby in short, simple sentences with a high pitch. While speaking to your baby, don't let another human voice or background noise distract

your baby.

- Motivate your baby to learn the words for the colors, sizes, and shapes of toys he is interested in. Always talk about what your baby is doing or experiencing, such as "You're drinking milk" or "You're playing with this brown teddy bear."
- Give your baby confidence to speak by not interrupting when he is about to say something, or putting words into his mouth. Let him say the words or what he wants to say.
- Use correct grammar and pronunciation whenever talking to your baby.
- Teach your baby the correct use of prepositions, such as *before*, *behind*, *inside*, *under*, as well as the use of connectives, such as *and, but, or, nor*.

Accelerate your baby's language learning to enhance his intellectual development, which is an important ingredient in his subsequent intelligence.

SEVEN

INCREASING INTELLIGENCE

Smartness is the capability of an individual to acquire and assimilate knowledge in multiple areas, to remember and store it, as well as to discover and develop potentiality in skills and talents. Smartness is the precursor to intelligence. In that respect, many of us are indeed smart because we are knowledgeable, gifted, and talented, as demonstrated by how quickly and efficiently we get things done, or how we can do certain activities better than someone else.

But are we intelligent? Or, what is IQ?

Intelligence and the Brain

IQ is more than just about acquisition and processing of knowledge and information by the brain; it is about the application of the information to solve problems or to achieve what the mind has set out to accomplish. Intelligence is smartness and beyond: it is about connecting all the dots together, and making sense of something that is apparently senseless and irrelevant.

To illustrate, a simple baby IQ test attests to a baby's intelligence in correctly identifying an object without seeing it after feeling the object hidden in a box; a smart baby is able to visually "see" what he touches. As a parent, you can play such similar games with your baby; the objective is not just to test his IQ but also to help his brain wired to that mode or mindset of "seeing what you touch," thereby instrumental in increasing his intelligence.

Increase intelligence by outsmarting the brain. Of course, the human brain is a very complex organ. The good news is that **Albert Einstein** had a fairly average brain size—only about 15 percent larger in areas responsible for visual-spatial recognition and math processing.

There are ways to grow and develop your baby's brain to increase his intelligence, which is a component of his genes, his environment, his experiences, his personality, and his upbringing.

Even if there are genes linked to high intelligence, they would be difficult to duplicate. Smart genes come from smart parents, who know how to provide the optimum environment for their babies to grow and develop their brains. An optimum environment means it is safe, secure, and stress-free to enjoy what he experiences, while subconsciously learns from those experiences, which become not only his personality and temperament but also his memories. All in all, your baby's upbringing holds the key to unlocking his intelligence and potentiality, and you as the parent always play a pivotal role.

Different Aspects of Intelligence

Information is the resource of human intelligence. If you wish your baby to be smart and intelligent, appreciate and enhance your baby's unique gifts.

Generally, there are several areas of intelligence demonstrated by babies and children even at an early age:

- *Language intelligence*: babies, showing a love for words and language, learn best by seeing, hearing, and saying words.
- *Spatial intelligence*: babies learn best by seeing things as where they are.
- *Kinesthetic intelligence*: babies with kinesthetic skills learn best through movement of different parts of the body.
- *Musical intelligence*: babies learn best with songs and melodies, or information put to music.
- *Logical intelligence*: babies who love abstract patterns and relationships between objects and things learn best with puzzles and games of logic.

As a parent, you need to not only recognize and explore your baby's unique gifts but also encourage the development of those special gifts inherent in your baby. Parents play a major role in the development of intelligence in a baby through the brain.

Remember, nobody is perfect. Despite his many physical disabilities, **President Theodore Roosevelt** was admitted to Harvard University at the age of 16, because he had a photographic memory and a deep desire to learn and to achieve.

Remember, nature controls your baby's intellectual development; there will be limits to what his brain can do, or what you as the parent can help. Your smart baby may show his intelligence in many different ways. Don't rely on IQ tests that your baby may later be exposed to. As a matter of fact, IQ tests were originally designed by a group of French psychologists to help and identify only those "mentally challenged" children in schools, and not the smart ones. Just as Harvard psychologist **Howard Gardner** said: "Strong evidence exists that the mind is a multi-faceted, multi-component instrument, which cannot in any legitimate way be captured in a single paper-and-pencil style instrument. Do what you can with what you have, and leave the rest to nature.

Essentials of Intelligence

Human intelligence includes certain key elements in the brain: curiosity; creativity; self-control; verbal communication; and non-verbal communication.

- Curiosity may kill a cat, but it will surely boost your baby's brain cells. Your baby must show his desire to explore and experience new things through his sensory organs; his brain cells must be able to expect certain results based on his own observation; his brain must then test and evaluate his expectation before he stores his acquired and verified information in the database of his brain. This whole mental process increases his brain cells by preparing him mentally to ask questions, such as "what if" and "why not," further down the road to intelligence. Arouse your baby's curiosity to know more, and gratify his desire with more know-how.
- Creativity is essential to intelligence in that it lets the mind think out of the preconditioned mindset to perceive new relationships between old things. It also involves a healthy dose of risk-taking, without

which the mind may become static and uncreative.

- Self-control or delayed self-gratification may also play a pivotal role in increasing intelligence over the long haul. Why? It is because distractions may be a stumbling block to learning; if your baby's brain can stay on task and say "no" to any unproductive distractions, he can increase his intelligence.

- Verbal communication skills play a pivotal role in the long-term development of intelligence. All babies have to learn the different sounds of the language they speak (phonemes), and understand the social implications of those words. Once the verbal skills of communication are acquired and mastered, learning in other areas will advance and accelerate Provide every opportunity to interact with your baby to teach him verbal skills to communicate with you.

- Nonverbal communication skills are as important as, if not more important than, the verbal ones in assessing human intelligence. The explanation is that nonverbal skills require the mental capability to read the mind of another by looking at the behavior and facial expression of that individual. Babies love to look at human faces. Give your baby every opportunity to study your face to develop his own nonverbal communication skill. According to psychologist **Paul Ekman**, all humans use similar facial muscles to express their similar emotions of anger, fear, sadness, and happiness, that is, their body language.

All in all, intelligence is the capability of the mind to

connect dots that are seemingly unconnected through creativity and imagination.

My Reflection

I remember how my daughter reacted when she saw me naked in the shower for the first time. She pointed at my private part, and said: "Daddy's pooh-pooh stool!" Up to now, my wife and I still find it amazingly funny in the way she connected the dots.

EIGHT

FINAL WORDS OF WISDOM

The Unique Gift

Your baby's coming into this world is already a miracle as well as a blessing. Be grateful for what you have—the unique gift from the Creator. In many ways, you are also the creator of this unique gift: you help him grow and develop; he is like the seed from nature, and you provide the air, the sunshine, the soil, and the water for him to grow and develop. No matter what, you are the parent, and the baby is yours forever. Make the best of this unique gift, and give your baby the most of what you have—your love, time, effort, and attention. Treasure this unique gift, and you will be blessed with joy and happiness for years to come.

The Importance of Time

Time will fly as your baby grows. Time is of essence because it shapes the future of your baby. There is a Chinese saying: "Age three defines what is up to eighty years old." The first three years of your baby are most important; they design his destiny and shape his future. Remember, you can never turn back the clock.

Of the first three years, the first year is the most important in the life of a baby: it defines his temperament and personality; it develops his brain cells; it forms the bonding with his parents. The first year is the only time to develop his multi-language skills and verbal talents. If you want your baby to speak more than one language or even multiple languages, give him the exposure within the first year, and don't procrastinate.

Time is of essence in that the more time you are willing to spend with your baby, the smarter he will become. It all depends on you, the parent.

The Changes and the Challenges

Your baby's arrival changes everything in your life: your relationships, your career, and, above all, your attitudes (how you look at everything and everyone around you). Challenges come with changes. To deal with these new life challenges, you need adaptability and compromise. For one thing, parenting priorities are always uniquely different in a couple. Make sure that both of you agree to disagree. The bottom line: a happy marriage always holds the key to raising a happy and smart baby. The birth of a baby should enhance and complement the marital relationship of a couple, and not putting any distance between them. No matter what, a single parent is always in a disadvantageous environment in raising a child. Welcome all challenges because they are also life-changing. Life is forever changing; a static life is not worth living, and this applies to your baby, as well as to you, the parent.

The Real and the Unreal

Your baby is living in a real world, and learning has to be real. Boosting your baby's language skills with language DVD is unreal; instead, your presence with your constant eye contact is real. Likewise, educational TV is no substitute for real human interactions. A plain cardboard box and crayons are real learning tools; they are far superior to expensive toys or high-tech learning devices and gadgets.

Telling your baby that he is smart is unreal in your baby's mind if he doesn't believe that he is really smart; worse, he may become unwilling to work on challenging problems. On the other hand, praising his effort is real for him.

The Happiness

A happy baby learns faster, and makes more friends when growing up. The importance of human relationships cannot be overstated; it plays a pivotal role in the future happiness of your baby. Knowing how to make friends and to keep friends is a lifelong skill that involves knowing when to interact and when to withdraw—that is, the capability to decipher nonverbal communication with others. To illustrate, while playing with your baby, if he turns away from you and starts sucking his thumb and staring into space, stop the play and wait for your baby's next response. If he turns to you again with an inviting smile, then resume the play.

As a parent, have the wisdom to decode the nonverbal communication of your baby. Babies can't talk, but by six months, most babies can experience anger, disgust, fear, happiness, surprise, and other emotions. Pay attention to the emotional landscape of your baby to understand his behavior, thereby instrumental in helping your baby develop his own nonverbal communication skills. Always verbalize your baby's emotions: "You're *happy*"; "You feel *surprised*, don't you?"; "I know you're *angry*." Verbalizing his emotions helps conveying your empathy, and thus calming the nerves of your baby. In addition, instill in your baby the attitude of gratitude.

Reading the minds of others to understand how they feel, and thereby instrumental in controlling one's own emotions, is critical to establishing good relationships with others, which is the source of happiness later in life.

No Expectation

Your baby's growth and development may be totally unpredictable. The milestones are just for your general reference; nothing is set in stone. Don't expect the expected, but always expect the unexpected.

Any disappointment or frustration will be reflected in the nonverbal communication that may be perceived by your baby. The bottom line: do what you can with what you have, and leave the rest to the Creator. If your baby is smart, you can make him super smart. On the other hand, if your baby is not as smart as you wish he were, you can still make him smarter that what he is now.

No matter what, you cannot do *everything*. After all, your baby has a life of his own; you cannot live his life *for* him. What he is going to encounter and experience further down the road in his life journey is beyond your control. As his parent, you can provide him with a compass and a roadmap. Along the journey, he is bound to run into detours, shortcuts, or may even get lost. Hopefully, with the right mindset and the wisdom you have instilled into his brain, he will get back on track and find his way to the destination that he has set for himself. Every life journey is a learning experience for that unique individual to learn and grow.

Learning What They Live and Living What They Learn

Babies, toddlers, children, teenagers, young adults—they all learn from what they live, and then live according to what they have learned.

- If a baby is often criticized, he will develop a judgmental temperament.
- If a baby often encounters angry outbursts, he will become aggressive, and even violent later in life.
- If a baby feels deprived and neglected, he will develop envy and jealousy, always comparing self with others.
- If a baby feels safe and secure, and being loved, he will demonstrate love and empathy towards others.
- If a baby experiences self-control, he will be patient and tolerant of others.
- If a baby is willing to share, he will develop an attitude of gratitude.

No matter what, all babies have their unique personalities and temperaments maturing at their own paces. Their "development risks" are affected and determined by their parents' own values and attitudes, as well as their own perceptions of what they have personally experienced.

What you, as a parent, can do is to teach your baby what you believe in, and express what you believe in through your own actions and interactions with your baby. How much your baby can absorb is entirely at his disposal. Nobody is perfect: you are not perfect, and neither will your baby be perfect. Therefore, have no expectation, and accordingly you have no stress for yourself or your baby!

The Power of Choice

Life is all about choices. The choices you make become your realities, which become your memories, and they often become the raw materials with which you weave the fabrics of your life. This is the reality of life.

Teach your baby the simple concept of choice, and reinforce it through everyday activities and games by always giving him the opportunity to choose between two or more things. This simple concept also underlies the idea of need and want; that is, he cannot have everything he wants—a very important life lesson to learn from the very beginning.

My Reflection

When my daughter was very young, I began teaching her the concept of choice, I often told her: "You're your choices."

Once at the traffic light while waiting to cross the road, I said to her: "God loves us and He protects us." She immediately responded by asking: "What if I cross the road right now, will God stop the car?" I asked her: "Will *you* cross the road?" She shook her head, and then I said: "You've a choice, and you're your choices." I didn't know if she understood me, but she nodded as if she did.

APPENDIX A

DEVELOPMENT REFERENCES

1st Month to 3rd Month

- While lying on his stomach, your baby lifts his head and chest.
- Your baby is aware of his right and left sides. Discovering his hands and feet, he stretches his limbs all the way out.
- Given a rattle, your baby holds it.
- Your baby sees within 10 inches. His eyes follow moving objects. He stares at objects or faces of people.
- Your baby responds to human voices and different sounds. Discovering different voices, qualities, and tones, he connects sounds and their sources.
- Your baby enjoys being touched by people or objects.
- Your baby responds to smile by smiling back.

4th Month to 6th Month

- Your baby stops using his tongue to push food out of his mouth, and develops the coordination to move solid food from the front of the mouth to the back for swallowing. (But wait until your baby is at least 6 months old before introducing solid foods, especially if your baby is exclusively breast-fed, in order to ensure that he gets the full health benefits of breast-feeding.)
- Your baby rolls over in both directions.
- Your baby wiggles forward on the floor.
- Your baby loves to play with his hands and feet.
- Your baby watches your mouth as you speak. He responds to verbal cues.
- Your baby likes to study human faces. He watches facial expressions.
- Your baby remembers things.
- Your baby responds to all stimulations of his senses.
- Your baby enjoys playing.
- Your baby understands taking turns.
- Your baby makes sounds.

7th Month to 9th Month

- Your baby bangs objects together. He reaches out for objects close by, and drags them to his side.
- Your baby points at things, and enjoys dropping things on purpose.
- Your baby gets up on all fours. He sits with little support. He crawls.
- Your baby makes two-syllable sounds. He learns the names of body parts and other things.

- Your baby is aware of body sounds. He enjoys nursery rhymes.

10th Month to 12th Month

- Your baby kicks and shakes his legs.
- Your baby masters his hand and finger coordination. He transfers things from one hand to the other, and then back. He enjoys putting things into boxes. He claps his hands, and waves goodbye.
- Your baby uses sign language to communicate.
- Your baby enjoys rolling balls back and forth.
- Your baby begins walking with help.
- Your baby likes to sing.
- Your baby laughs at funny things.
- Your baby begins his speech, saying two-syllable words. He understands the meaning of words in context. He not only understands but also follows simple instructions.
- Your baby copies and imitates your actions.
- Your baby understands cause and effect.
- Your baby likes to look at books and pictures.
- Your baby responds to questions with actions or words.
- Your baby likes to "pretend."

For a new baby, there is always the first time for everything. However, the "first times" may vary because each baby is unique. Your baby is constantly changing. The development references are not set in stone; they are intended to give you some idea as to what you can expect from your baby each month, well as what you can do to encourage your baby's progress. Use the development references to gain insight into what you are observing in your baby today, and to preview what you can look forward to in the months ahead.

APPENDIX B

SIMPLE GAMES

Simple games are just interactions with your baby to stimulate his physical growth, as well as his emotional, social, and intellectual development. The human brain is complex, especially that of a baby, which is 250 percent more active than that of an adult. Activity in the brain creates synapses, which are electrical connections responsible for the complex wiring system within the brain. The number of synapses in the brain is directly related to the number of stimulations it receives, especially within the first three years, in particular, the first twelve months. Remember, the networking of the synapses is almost complete after the first three years. Therefore, time is of essence as far as stimulations are concerned. The more connections your baby's brain has, the more intelligent he becomes.

You need simple games to stimulate the complex brain of your baby. Simplicity is the key to learning complex matters. The following is a list of simple games. Always use your imagination and creativity to play games with your baby.

1ˢᵗ Month to 3ʳᵈ Month

- Make soft and gentle sounds with a toy in your hands close to your baby. Let your baby hear the sounds, touch the toy, and grasp it.
- Help your baby mimic your different facial expressions, such as smiling, blinking, and closing your eyes, and sticking out your tongue. Do this while you are feeding, diapering, or bathing him.
- Explore different types of touch on your baby to stimulate his different sensory organs. You can use a straw and blow air on his skin, or roll a small, soft ball up and down his body. Touch plays a pivotal role in your baby's cognitive and immunological development.
- Hold your baby and place him with his tummy on an inflated ball. This stimulates him to lift his head and chest, and thereby strengthening his neck muscles.
- Gently shake and move a rattle from right to left, and then from left to right, to let your baby's eyes follow it. This helps your baby connecting the right and left hemispheres of his brain. Alternatively, you can move your fingers up and down within 10 inches of your baby's eyes. This also develops your baby's tracking skills.
- Move your baby's legs up and down, as well as sideways, by cupping his feet in the palms of your hands to strengthen his leg muscles.
- Place your baby in new places and new positions so that he can see you from different angles to increase his visual scope and stimulation.
- Hold your baby and speak to him in a sing-song

voice, or an animated voice. This stimulates the orbitofrontal cortex of his brain, according to a neuroscientist.

- Use different signs of sign language to communicate with your baby, such as "go to *sleep*," "you're *hungry*," and "you want *milk*." At around eight to ten months, your baby will be able to use simple sign language to reciprocate.
- Identify the voice you should use to communicate with your baby. Call his name several times, using different voices, from high to low. See your baby's response to your different voices. Identify the voice that your baby likes best, and use that voice.
- Increase the neuron-to-neuron connections within your baby's brain by talking to him as often as possible; according to experts, these connections are responsible for your baby's first spoken word. Speak slowly with pauses in between; emphasize key words; use short sentences; maintain constant eye contact while speaking. If your baby says "ma," then you say "ma. . .ma-ma," and if he says "ba," then you say "ba. . .ba-bottle."
- In the beginning, your baby recognizes only black, white, and red. Introduce your baby to other brightly colored toys, such as blue, green, yellow, and purple.
- Introduce the concept of back and forth. Paste a picture of a toy or fun animal on a white paper plate; show the side with the picture and then the side without the picture. Repeat this back and forth.
- Hold your baby and dance to some soothing music to help your baby remember the soft and soothing

movement inside the womb.

- Your baby's sense of smell is well developed at birth. Enhance his sense of smell by giving him, for example, a banana, to smell to further develop his preferences for certain smells.

4th Month to 6th Month

- Help your baby practice crawling. Place a toy a few inches in front of your baby lying on his tummy. Your baby will want to crawl towards it. Gently press your hands on his feet so that he will have to push against the pressure. To further reinforce your baby's crawling capability, lie down on the floor, and let your baby crawl all over you. Crawling enhances cross patterning activities to prepare him for walking.
- Help your baby roll over. Place your baby on his tummy on a towel. Slowly and carefully roll him over to one side, while using your hand to guide him.
- Increase your baby's neck muscles and head control by bouncing him a "ride": place a towel over one of your knees, and seat your baby over your knee, while gently bouncing him up and down.
- Your baby's hearing develops rapidly in the first few months. Help him develop his discrimination between sounds by tapping different objects on different surfaces, clapping your hands, snapping your fingers, whistling, or just playing a musical instrument. Your baby's awareness of sounds is the foundation of his language learning.

- If your baby babbles, wait and pause, and then respond by mimicking his babble. Wait for your baby to babble again. Do the same if he coos, gurgles, and squeals. You are teaching your baby the art of conversation, which is taking turns.
- Before you do anything to your baby, always tell him what you are going to do, and thus giving him verbal cues to help him understand the language.
- To develop your baby's memory, teach him simple sign language. Make signing with your baby a natural part of your daily activities. Reinforce your baby's memory with games showing him how things appear, disappear, and reappear.

7th Month to 9th Month

- Roll a ball back and forth between you and your baby to help him focus, reach accurately for objects, as well as develop his fine and large motor skills.
- Teach your baby to drag objects towards him: let your baby hold one end of a towel while sitting up; show your baby how to pull his end of the towel; move your body towards your baby, making him feel that he has pulled you towards him.
- Show your baby how to purse his lips together and blow air out. Stack up cards and let your baby blow them down to teach him cause and effect.
- Your baby enjoys dropping things on purpose as soon as he perceives the concept of cause and effect. Don't forget to name the objects he has dropped, and verbalize his action.
- While looking in the mirror with your baby, clap

and wave your hands, stick out your tongue, and make facial expressions to see if your baby mimics you.

- Your baby loves to point at objects. Imitate him while repeating the names of those objects he is pointing at.
- Your baby is increasingly aware of different parts of his body. Make different sounds with different parts of his body to make him more aware of sounds and the names of the parts of his body.

10th Month to 12th Month

- Lie down on your back with your baby next to you, and then wiggle, kick, and shake your legs; ask your baby to mimic you.
- Show your baby how a zipper works on a piece of clothing. His practice strengthens his thumb and forefinger coordination. With better coordination, show your baby how to transfer an object from one hand to the other, and then back.
- Look at books with your baby, showing him pictures to encourage his language development. Comment on the details of the pictures to engage his attention as well as to increase his vocabulary development.
- Teach your baby the sign language of "more" to make him understand that with sign or language he can convey what he wants. Reinforce the use of the sign "more" in everyday activities.
- Teach your baby simple instructions, such as "show me your hand," "touch your nose," "wave bye-bye.".

ABOUT STEPHEN LAU

His websites, blog, and newsletter:

- http://www.stephencmlau.com

- http://www.wisdominliving.com

- http://www.booksbystephenlau.com

- http://reflectionsofstephenlau.blogspot.com

- http://www.wellness-wisdom-newsletter.com

His recommendations:

- Fields, Denise, and Brown, Ari, M.D., *Baby 411*, 5th Edition, Ingram Publishing Services

- Smart, Sally, *The Dos and Don'ts During Pregnancy*, Amazon, Kindle

- http://www.brillbaby.com

www.ingramcontent.com/pod-product-compliance
Lightning Source LLC
Chambersburg PA
CBHW050428290526
45786CB00003B/1447